MY JOURNEY
TO THE STARS

ASTRONAUT
SCOTT KELLY

WITH EMILY EASTON

ILLUSTRATIONS BY **ANDRÉ CEOLIN**

Crown Books for Young Readers ♕ New York

ACKNOWLEDGMENTS

I would like to thank Emily Easton for collaborating on this book. It's my first children's book, and it couldn't have been a better experience thanks to her. Many thanks to the very talented André Ceolin for the great illustrations. My literary agent, Elyse Cheney, has been so much more to me than a literary agent, advisor, mentor, and friend, so thank you, Elyse! Thanks to my grown-up partner, Amiko Kauderer, and my childhood partner, Mark Kelly, for their assistance in many areas of this book. I also want to thank my two kids, Samantha and Charlotte, for looking over the manuscript and saying, "That's awesome!" Ana Guzman was critical to organizing the 500,000 photos I have from my year in space. Without her assistance, my job of finding the right photos would have been nearly impossible.

PICTURE CREDITS

Key: t—top, b—bottom, c—center, l—left, r—right

Dr. Jorge Cartes and Tim Gagnon: 2; Mark Kelly: 37 (t); Scott Kelly: 4, 8 (tl, tr, bl), 14, 29 (b); NASA: 6, 8 (br), 17, 27, 32, 33 (t, b), 34, 35, 36, 37 (b), 38, 40 (t, c, br), 44, 46; NASA/Bill Ingalls: 47 (t, b), back cover; NASA/Scott Kelly: front and back jacket flaps, 41, 45 (t, b); NASA/Robert Markowitz: 1; NASA/Tim Peake: 43; NASA/Stephanie Stoll: 5; Star-Ledger Photographs © The Star-Ledger, Newark, NJ: 20, 21; SUNY Maritime College: 29 (t); Jerry P. Tarnoff: 23; US Navy/VF-143—The World Famous Pukin' Dogs: 30–31.

Text copyright © 2017 by Mach 25 LLC

Jacket art and interior illustrations copyright © 2017 by André Ceolin

All rights reserved. Published in the United States by Crown Books for Young Readers, an imprint of Random House Children's Books, a division of Penguin Random House LLC, New York.

Crown and the colophon are registered trademarks of Penguin Random House LLC.

Visit us on the Web! randomhousekids.com

Educators and librarians, for a variety of teaching tools, visit us at RHTeachersLibrarians.com

Library of Congress Cataloging-in-Publication Data

Names: Kelly, Scott, 1964– | Ceolin, Andre, illustrator.

Title: My journey to the stars / Scott Kelly ; illustrated by Andre Ceolin.

Description: New York : Crown Books for Young Readers, [2017] |

Audience: Age 5–8. | Audience: K to grade 3.

Identifiers: LCCN 2017011226 | ISBN 978-1-5247-6377-0 (hc) |

ISBN 978-1-5247-7031-0 (glb) | ISBN 978-1-5247-6379-4 (ebook)

Subjects: LCSH: Kelly, Scott, 1964– | Astronauts—United States—

Biography—Juvenile literature. | International Space Station.

Classification: LCC TL789.85.K45 K45 2017 | DDC 629.450092 [B]—dc23

Book design by Nicole de las Heras

MANUFACTURED IN CHINA

10 9 8 7 6 5 4 3 2 1

First Edition

To my daughters,
Samantha and Charlotte

It's been 340 days since I set foot on Earth. I've spent almost a full year living and working on the International Space Station (ISS). It's the hardest thing I've ever done.

I miss fresh air and the feel of rain on my face. I miss hugging my daughters and my girlfriend, Amiko.

At last, it's time to get into the spaceship that will take me home.

I say my goodbyes to the team who has become my space family. Then I climb into my seat.

The spaceship is so small my knees are folded against my chest. My two Russian crewmates sit so close to me, our elbows touch.

We all strap ourselves in tight.

It's going to be a **WILD RIDE!**

My perfect copy—my identical twin—is waiting for me back on Earth. My brother, Mark, and I are the only twins in NASA history.

We were born on February 21, 1964, in Orange, New Jersey, and grew up in West Orange, the same town where Thomas Edison made many of his inventions.

Mark was born six minutes before me. Since then, we have spent our lives as partners, always ready for adventure.

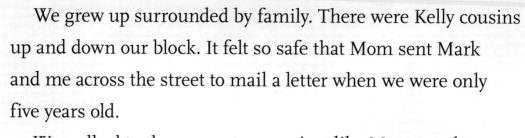

We grew up surrounded by family. There were Kelly cousins up and down our block. It felt so safe that Mom sent Mark and me across the street to mail a letter when we were only five years old.

We walked to the corner to cross just like Mom taught us. After we mailed the letter, I walked back to the corner. But Mark, always a daredevil, crossed in the middle of the street.

Then I got the scare of my life . . . my brother was hit by a car!

SCREEEEEECH!

Mark hurt his head. He was rushed to the hospital, while
I had to stay with our uncle Joe and eat liver for dinner. *Yuck!*
Mark got better and came home with a great story. I felt like I
got the worse deal.

Mark and I always had a talent for finding trouble and taking risks. Sometimes we got hurt. But every time we took a risk, we pushed our limits and aimed higher.

This was great training for the biggest risk of all—*becoming astronauts!*

Every weekend, Mark and I stayed with Grandma and
Pop Pop so Mom and Dad could go out.

We loved our special routine—breakfast at a local diner
and a day trip. New Jersey is the Garden State, and there were
always amazing gardens to visit. Years later, I'd think about
Grandma and Pop Pop as I took care of the flowers on the ISS.

At home, every day was different. Our parents didn't always get along. We never knew when a fight might start. It was scary when they argued. Mark and I would hide in our room.

Watching our parents fight turned Mark and me into
peacemakers. We can get along with almost anyone.
We learned to stay calm in the toughest of times. This has
helped us each lead our own crews in space.

Dad was a police officer. When I was eleven years old,
Mom decided to become a police officer too. In the 1970s,
police departments had just started to let women join the force.
But first they had to pass the same test that men did.

My parents may have fought a lot, but Dad still had Mom's
back. He set up a training course in our backyard.

I agreed to be Mom's practice dummy, pretending to be hurt so she could drag me to safety.

The hardest part of the course was the wall Mom had to climb. Every day, she tried to climb over that wall. At first, she couldn't even touch the top. It took Mom a long time, but she finally did it.

Soon after, Mom passed the test and became one of the first female cops in New Jersey! Her success showed Mark and me that if we had a plan, with small steps we could turn a big dream into something real.

A REAL-LIFE POLICE STORY

I still didn't know what my dream was. I was a terrible
student. I couldn't sit still. I couldn't listen to the teacher.
And I couldn't stop watching the squirrels out the window.

Even so, Mr. Tarnoff, my principal, believed in me.
He begged me not to give up. And years later, he was
invited to both my space shuttle launches.

During high school, Mark and I joined the volunteer ambulance unit. Every night was different. We never knew what to expect. And riding in the ambulance, sirens screaming, was exciting. Most important, we liked helping people.

I had finally found something I loved. I wanted to become a doctor. But how was I ever going to get through college and medical school when I could barely sit still?

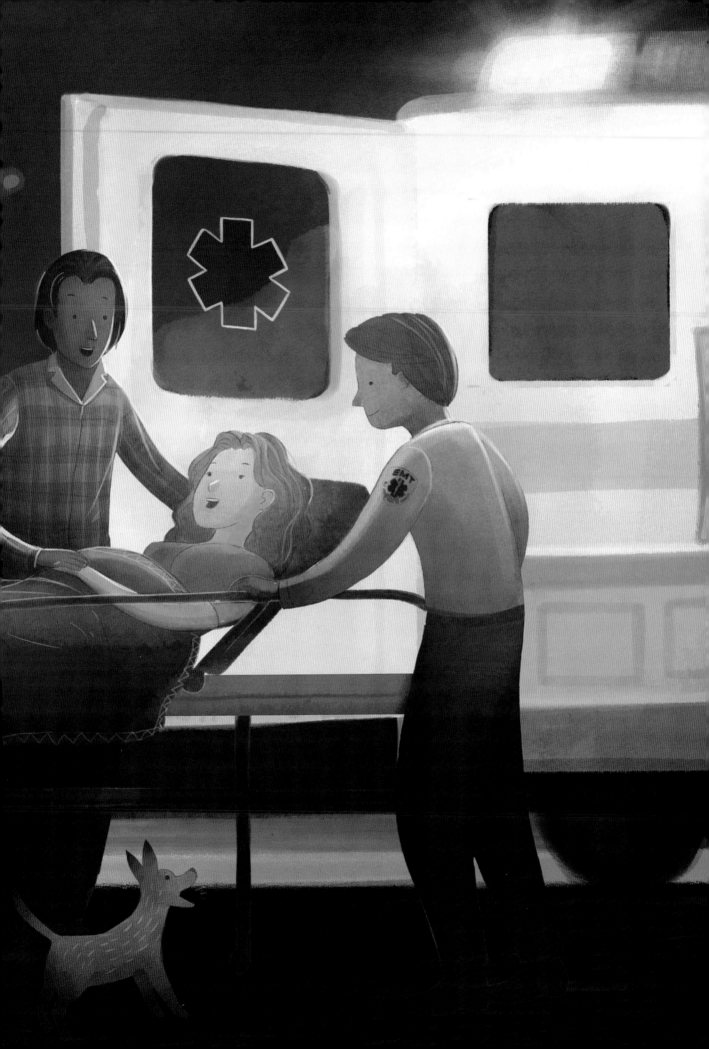

One day, I went to the bookstore to buy gum and a book cover caught my eye. It was *The Right Stuff* by Tom Wolfe.

"Pick me up! Open me!" it called.

That book changed my life *forever*. It was so exciting, full of daring pilots risking everything to test the newest planes.

How **FAST** could they go?

How **HIGH** could they fly?

Sometimes pilots **CRASHED**.

Sometimes they **SOARED**.

The best became the Mercury Seven,
the first NASA astronauts.

I finally found my dream! I wanted to be a test pilot.
And thanks to Mom, I knew how to make my dream real.
I would create my plan. I would follow it step by step.
STEP ONE: Do my homework. Now that I had a goal,
I was able to work hard and graduate from college.

STEP TWO: Join the navy. Here I could learn how to fly. Mark started flight school too.

I quickly learned that flying fast was fun! But it wasn't easy.

I took a lot of risks as a jet pilot. I needed to see how fast my plane could fly and how good a pilot I could be.

Flying a fighter jet was so hard. The first time I tried to land on a moving ship, I couldn't do it.

But I didn't give up. In the end, I flew faster than the speed of sound.

Then I was unstoppable. I wanted to fly higher and higher. To do that, I needed to go to space.

MARK   SCOTT

We each flew into space four times. We flew on space shuttles, a Russian spaceship called the Soyuz, and the ISS. But we never went to space together in case something went wrong.

Space travel was our biggest risk of all!

NASA's next big mission is to send astronauts to Mars. First they need to see what happens when human bodies are in space for a long time.

Twin astronauts were perfect for this job. So NASA asked me to spend a full year in space. No American had ever stayed in space that long.

One twin astronaut in space—me—tested his brain, blood, eyes, muscles, and bones. One twin on Earth—Mark—did the same tests. NASA will continue to study us over time and compare the results.

After my year in space, I stretched almost two inches and my eyesight got worse. But I am mostly back to normal now.

MARK ON EARTH

SCOTT IN SPACE

Living on the ISS is very different from living on Earth. There's no gravity, so you float around. Floating sounds like fun, and it is. But tools you are using float away—and that can be so annoying! Even your body can float away when you are sleeping.

That's why the crew has to sleep in bags that hang on the wall or ceiling, drink through a special straw, and use a special bathroom that is like a vacuum cleaner.

My crew on the ISS was so busy. NASA told us what to do all day so we could fit everything in. They told us when to eat, when to exercise, and when to work in the lab.

We had four hundred experiments to run. Many of them studied the effects of zero gravity on the lab rats—the crew and the twenty mice on board.

We even grew plants in space. I liked to water the flowers. It reminded me of seeing gardens with Grandma and Pop Pop. I liked eating the lettuce even more. We were the first crew to eat fresh vegetables grown on the ISS.

NASA did its best to keep our crew safe. But the ISS is at risk every minute. Our crew faced *extra* dangers during my year in space. First, we lost two unmanned ships bringing fresh food and supplies when one crashed in April and another exploded in June.

Second, the ISS was almost hit and destroyed by space junk in July.

And third, we had to make an emergency space walk to fix the ISS in December.

Earth meant everything to the crew while we were so far away. We loved to look out the windows at our beautiful planet. From our perch 220 miles above Earth, we saw big cities glittering in the blackness of night and the sun shining on rivers and oceans in many brilliant shades of blue. Our crew wanted to share the beauty. We hoped our photos would inspire people to help protect our amazing home.

HOUSTON

NEW ORLEANS

THE BAHAMAS

Finally, my mission is done. It feels good to know that all the risks I've taken have brought humans one step closer to Mars.

Now it's time to go home. Our Soyuz capsule is falling back to Earth at almost one thousand feet per second. Gravity presses down on us. It's hard to breathe. It feels like going over Niagara Falls in a barrel—but while you're on fire!

The parachute opens. The landing is so hard my head slams into the seat cushion. Then the hatch opens and strong arms help me out.

The fresh air smells amazing!

NASA pokes and prods me. After many tests, I'm cleared to return to Texas. I land in Houston and give my whole family a big bear hug. When I get home, I walk straight to my yard and jump in the pool with all my clothes on. The sights, smells, and sounds of Earth surround me.

My year in space ends with my first shower and first night's sleep in a bed since I left for the ISS.

AHHHHHH . . .

What an amazing journey!